The Spinning Place The Spinning Place

Also by Chelsea Wagenaar

*Mercy Spurs the Bone*

# The Spinning Place

Chelsea Wagenaar

*Winner of the 2018 Michael Waters Poetry Prize*

Published by the University of Southern Indiana
Evansville, Indiana

ISBN: 978-1-930508-47-7 First Edition

Printed in the USA

Library of Congress Control Number: 2019947432

This publication is made possible by the support of the Indiana Arts Commission, the National Endowment for the Arts, the University of Southern Indiana College of Liberal Arts, the USI English Department, the USI Foundation, and the USI Society for Arts & Humanities.

*Southern Indiana Review* Press
Orr Center #2009
University of Southern Indiana
8600 University Boulevard
Evansville, Indiana 47712

*sir.press@usi.edu*
*usi.edu/sir*
Ron Mitchell & Marcus Wicker, eds.

Cover art: *Solace*; © 2019 Deedra Ludwig; *deedraludwig.com*
Cover design: Zach Weigand
Layout: Megan Miller

*to Eloise & Hopkins*

# CONTENTS

## —The First Spinning—

## —Fields of Praise—

*So it must have been after the birth of the simple light*
*In the first, spinning place, the spellbound horses walking warm*
*Out of the whinnying green stable*
*On to the fields of praise.*

–Dylan Thomas, "Fern Hill"

## —The First Spinning—

# THE SPINNING PLACE

*Mars rotates on its axis, completing one revolution every 24.6 hours.*
–NASA

Think of something you wish we had
a word for, I tell my students.
If our experience flows through the current
of language, then how do we live
what we cannot say? What would you say
if you could? A student says, a word for longing
for someone who is in the same room.
A word for the particular quiet of the house
just after loved ones leave, the spare bed
disheveled, extra cups by the sink,
alluvial silt of tea still warm in the porcelain.
One girl raises her hand:
a word for the way we feel when people sing
"Happy Birthday" to us.
*Yes*—that annual blend of pleasure
and embarrassment, the sombrero
tilted on your head while the other patrons
look up from their salted rims,
the birthday candles beading blue wax while dad
pans the camera around the glowing faces.
I last heard the song four months ago
just as my daughter pushed free of me.
Dr. Wilson began to sing, the surprise of his baritone
rising in the midst of both our cries,
*Happy birthday, dear Eloise*...her face purple
and swollen, the slick curling cord that bound us
then cut. I have often wondered what the doctor said
when my sister gave birth to twins, one alive
and one not. No song or word can sing
into that abyssal joy, that sorrow. A word for the prayer
of pure praise wedded to sheer anguish. A word
for longing for someone who is in the same body.

How often I'd longed for my daughter
those nine months, even as she turned and stirred
beneath my hands, only as far away
as my skin is deep. Perhaps there is no word
that is *not* longing. When my sister and I
are silent together on the phone,
I can't help but think of the Mars Rover,
280 million miles away rolling slowly
through a crater of red rock and dust,
singing "Happy Birthday" to itself.
This is how my sister will always feel
when she sings that song to her son—
both elegy and ode, a tune that rises
from a dark depth no one else
can know. A word for praise
struck from the flint of sorrow. A word for longing
for someone who is in the same cosmos.
A word for the look of the earth
as glimpsed from Mars, twinned in its spinning,
unsayable and green in its faraway light.

# Annunciation (While Pregnant, I Develop Aviophobia)

It wasn't when the test read *yes*, or when the blood
    didn't come, or when my breasts

became so tender I shrank even from the shower's
    hot-fingered caress. No, I first became convinced

of our two helical strands spiraling & knotting
    inside me beyond my ability to count or stop them

only when, as the plane nosed west somewhere over Georgia,
    my skin paled, lit with a cold, fevered sheen of panic,

made of me a trembling hallucination. All sound
    reached me as through a blue whelm of sea,

a high, keening whale call. Alone among strangers,
    my body glyphed with secret & threatening to tell,

I slipped from consciousness into the stewardess's
    firm grip on my elbow, the oxygen mask

she cupped over my face, her waterwords calling
    *Is there a doctor on board?* I fell & fell

from that sky, unearthly, impossibly winged, to find you
    in the airport, my oracle's lips lusterless.

But I brought you no prophecy at all,
    only a kind of proof of what had already happened:

my clothes still cloud-dewed with sweat, my hair
    tendriled damply to my neck with the labor

of what it took to descend with this news.

# Prelude to Circulatory System

There was the pelican who snagged
her feet in the ocean,
& white gulls that clotted near crusts
of foam. Before that, a blindfold
of cloud stretched from horizon ear
to ear. Before that, the moon
on the tesseral water. Cuban bread
& Spanish wine. A stand that sold
gourmet popsicles. A word
in my throat when I looked at him.
The sigh of sheets on the line,
the sigh of sheets moving & still
with us. Perhaps I've gone too far—
the distance between *begin* & *begun*
is the upturned world before
the retina translates. Already I'm too late.
Already you have moved
from your fallopian dark
to the blooded sanctum where you root.
The earthly currents begin to swish
through you. It is as though
my skin is an eave against which
a curled bird begins to stir.

## Scale

*I am soft sift*
*In an hourglass*
—Gerard Manley Hopkins

Against the darkening winterplum sky,
a lone contrail whitens—loose thread, untufted
cotton. A perfect inverse of me:
Lenten moon

of my belly taut, halved by a slurred gray line.
*Linea nigra,* the doctor says, my belly button's
new ashen tail a ghostly likeness of the cut cord

that once bound me to my mother.
These days I am a solstice, a season begun
in your germinal dark. Measure me now

in months, in so many weeks, all the streams
of my body downrivering
into the estuary that is you.
That is you—

there, the tick of your limbs, a second hand,
a second hand, fingers whorled and filling
with bone, numbered one by one,

as are your days in that luminous Book.
Nameless one, I know you in numbers.
Your parts, your gathering weeks, the count

of your heart. The thrum of kicks
in an hour is as many as the sparrows
that flit in the bare snarl of vine and hedge,

as many as the houses that line our street,
my trips to the bathroom in the night.
I think, in those small, bleary hours,

of the hand that pens the book of our days,
turns the page. Nameless one, only once more
will you be numberless, when you begin

again. Day you quicken toward, cold sear
of light, fugue of voices. You'll be cut
like yarn from the skein, your skin unshined

of blood, your heels grasped and slapped.
Cry, numberless one—for now you are laid
upon the scale, the eye of its zero

the first to blink.

# Descent (Sort of an Annunciation)

At the tree's tip the hawk folds
his massive dust-colored wings
and casts his yellow eyes
like a line upon the fields,
crisp and blue in the season's first frost.
He is not a dove,
though when he descends
it will be with the velocity
of van Eyck's dove
toward Mary's crown.
The cars on this highway
do not slow to look.
The world is always moving,
and nearly everything in it.
There was morning,
and there was evening, the story goes.
And the animals, and the man's tongue
in his strange mouth naming them.
The first work is to speak.
Why, then, when I saw you
in your shadowclouds
on the screen, webbed and froglike,
your one heart a nucleus
of trembling—why could I not?
Perhaps that is what the hawk's eye
roves for—how it knows what unstill thing
to pursue. (I was afraid. Afraid of our oneness,
my ability to save you
from nothing.) And finding the quickening
in the smallest grassblade shadow
it dives, a descent upon which
everything depends, morning and evening
and the name of the creature
in the crosshairs of that yellow eye,
now terrified
into the rest of its life.

# Poison

Thrash of feet through thorns,
        mangled undergrowth, away
    from the voice calling *one, two, three*—

we shattered out from *base,*
        the seeker's cantor ascending
    the numeric scale,

we hiders seeking vine enclave,
        chokecherry cloister,
    fox hollow, a banishment

we exulted in, to see
        but not be seen. Days later,
    my mother would know

where I'd been—archipelagos of red
        hived along my arms
    and neck, fleeted across my belly,

ankle, thigh. I was an agony of skin
        and calamine, yes—
    how I longed in the damp nights

for my sheets to snuff my body's
        interminable guttering—
    but I would suffer again

that trinity of leaves—its honest touch—
        over yours, traceless
    and secret, incurable.

# My Sister Sketches Her Anorexia

The nude girl on the page looks away,
knees sharp as the corners of rooms,
ribs a legible alphabet of bone.
But the drawn girl does not know
what it is to refuse to eat—
she was born this way
from my sister's coal pencil. Suppose
this is how we arrived here,
already advanced in our renunciations,
already granted the ruins of ourselves.
Imagine the nurse in her blood-smattered blues,
weeping a little to lay the starving baby
on the scale. Would we be happy then?—
sainted errata, wounds anticipating
wounds? The mother would stretch
out her arms with umbilical love
to hold the crying anatomy of air,
who, in a few years will sketch her
hungered self. Now see the drawn girl
twist to look at her own delible edges.
See her scratch at them with her thumbnails.
How she works to erase herself.

## Advent

Last week a jellied disc
in one of my husband's lower vertebrae
cinched, slipped—on the x-ray
the bones' thorned edges gritted against each other,
his whole spine yearning left,
a lily stem arched toward the promise
of light. Now the days shrink
into themselves, the trees bare-limbed
but for squirrels' nests and the green
bloom of mistletoe, the opalescent berries
suspended like droplets of milk.
All my comforts are questions:
*Is it better, does this help?* and to wonder
at the body as host, his to pain,
mine to our firstborn. Unseen, unfelt
arms and legs push into socket,
joints form, the elbow a door
swinging open. Before you, before your
cloistral assembly of parts, I knew
words waiting to become you:
*face, hair, cuticle.* Was it this way
for Mary, overshadowed by the Spirit?—
her body not hers, reworded with the promise
of flesh? *How can this be?* I echo her,
though I have known a man.
*Here?* I ask him, and soothe cream
into his skin, the two divots in the small
of his back—gates that keep the invisible hurt.
*May it be as you have said—*
and I picture her trembling hands,
the hour dusk, everything vague and blued,
hour all the shadows become shadow.

# Solstice

It's obscurity inscribed on the air,
birch limbs unlit one by one,
the moon a blurted secret at both ends
of the day. The opossum revel and slink
with nothing but moon and eyeglow
to illumine tossed cans and wrappers.
*I could ask the darkness to hide me,*
the psalmist wrote, and this day would seem
the answer, the wild approaching dark barely fronded
with light: firs mantled in white dust,
windows crypted with frost. Anna told me
about those girls, what their stepfather did to them.
Milton—going blind as he wrote
*Paradise Lost*—imagined that in hell
not even the fires give off light.
*But even in darkness I cannot hide from you.*
Some stories are too true to finish.
Some darks too dark. Across the way,
blackbirds fling upward from a field,
their bodies fluent with ascent.
Beneath each wing a startling ember:
last light carried off
into the deepening firmament.

## Lines Approaching a Birthday

Days of rain. Days of rain on piles

of plowed snow spumed black
with grit.
                    Then, diluted sun and peony-
rumor, still unmoved in their silk slumber.

For a long time I believed the right words
could make a thing beautiful.

Maybe so: there is the low white
plaster of cloud, February's unexalted

architecture.
                         It will open soon,
into blue rib vault, and I with it,

open the way a spade
                                        opens earth.

The way a crane opens a church.

Sleep for now, child,
like the tulip bulbs tucked
                                              in their dormant dark,
sounded by cold rain.

You by my chandelier heart.

# Delivery Room (Sacrament Under Erasure)

*Matthew 26:23-29*

Who has his hand?<br>
   Betray me, son,<br>
 just written.

Who would be better   if  born?

 I answered,   you—

gave and broke and gave<br>
         my body,<br>
   offered it to<br>
       you,  my blood<br>
 poured out for<br>
   you.

       Drink of this.<br>
   Now drink

anew,   you,<br>
       my kingdom.

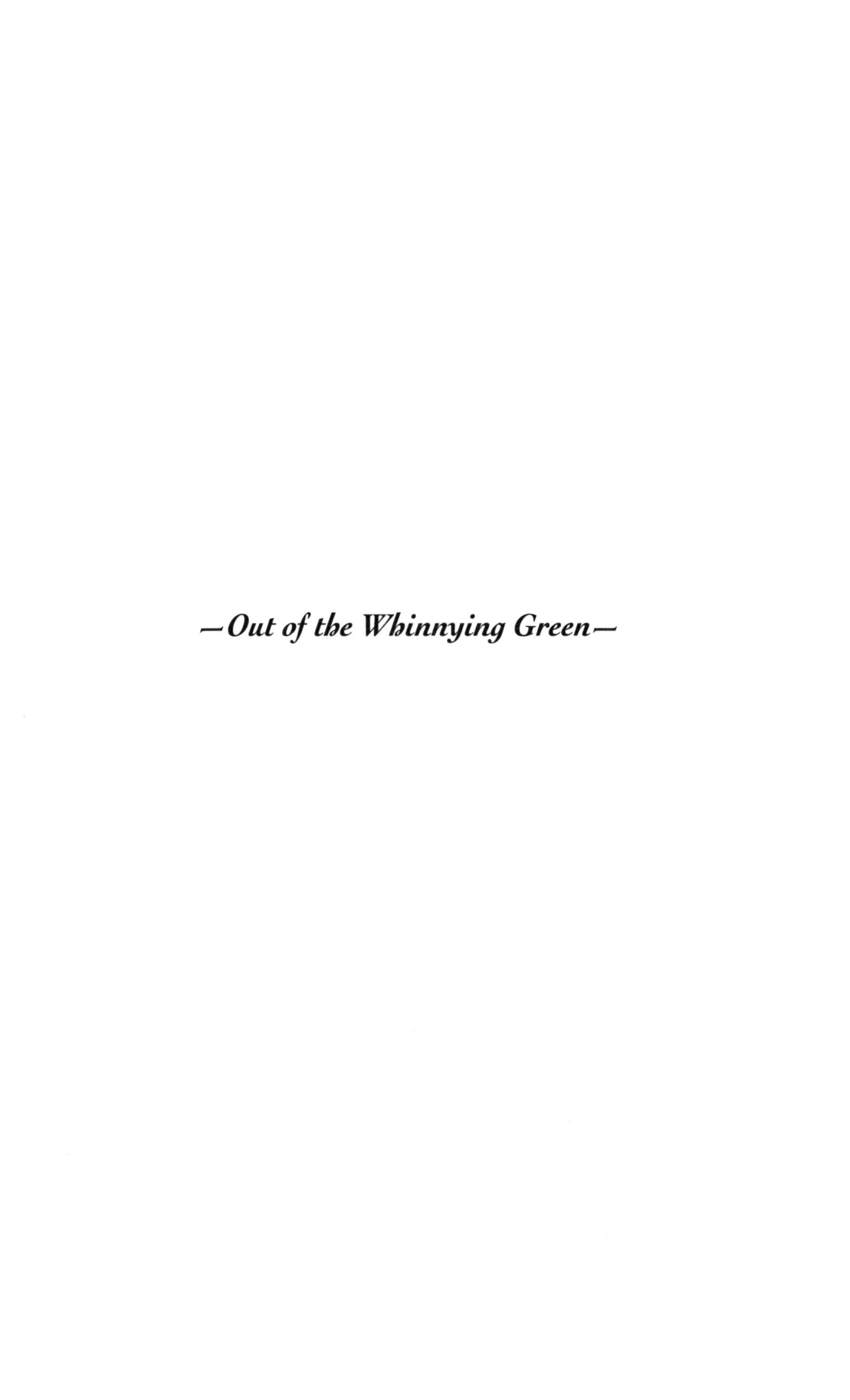

# —Out of the Whinnying Green—

# Exile (The Spellbound Horses)

In a field, a house.

Asleep in the house, a girl dreams,
but this is not the dream.

From the barn behind the house, nervous whinnying,
the safe smell of shit and hay.

Blue lupine rims the whole field, bends
in a crescendo of wind,
then another and another.

A dark cone twists from the low clouds,
arrows earthward,
spins toward the whinnying.

In the dream the girl is speaking
but her words collapse into garbled sounds
and someone she loves steps farther away
until he can no longer hear her.

The horses are silent now,
black as pupils, a mime of fright

even as the dark cone shreds the roof
of their barn, the partition between their stalls.
Now the walls, too, are hoisted and heaved

into jagged planks about the yard,
and the hay whirls into a seething cloud of whips
to send them from this place.

Afterward,
in the calm and ruined wake
the horses are free—
they can cross together the field's lupine edge
alone as gods,
free as exiles.

And the sleeping girl, when will she know their sorrow?

When she wakes
she will find the end of the world
is the shape of the absence of two horses
switching their tails beyond what she can see.

In the ravaged yard her feet will be bare, her hair uncombed,
and the sugar will slip through her fingers.

# Miscarriage

*for C*

The bleeding began the night of the first blood moon
in five years. Slow, rutilant, your dark womb

emptied: arils spilled from the fruit. Pod slipped
from the husk that held it. All night you kept

close to the bathroom's white sear. You thought
the tinged moon wanted free; it twisted, caught

in your windowed sky. A larger body hid it from light.
(Yours. *Yours. Oh God let it not be right.*)

Who mutinied? Progesterone, antibodies?
Corpus luteum? *No body. No, body,*

*it's not a foreign object.* The hours pulsed a deeper sanguine
until the alignment broke. Your grief scene

diminished to white tile, flushing water. And the stars
(small as poppy seeds) flared the huge dark,

gave it a shape and a name.

## Night Shift

Moon-sliced, streetlit blear,
coal train moving
like its own ghost along the tracks.
Two a.m., three a.m., my shadow sways
as I catch myself, hand on the wall,
pulled from bed by your nocturnal haunt,
you at your crib rail, blanket clutched,
more sound than body.
*There, there. Shh. Shh.*
You tremble against me: to nightmare
without language, no way to tell me
who chased you, drowned you, snatched you
from my cart when I turned my back:
isn't this a version of hell?
Ah, but these are *my* nightmares.
Yours are locked from me in the crypt
of your mind, which expands even now
toward syntax, memory.
Forgive me: I begrudge you these hours.
St. Paul wrote of those who had fallen
asleep in the Lord, sleep our foretaste
of Sleep. Little crier, wild yawp sounding
the halls, calling me awake,
this is your rehearsal.
One day your sound will not resurrect me.
I deceive you,
climbing from the earth each night,
shaking off the tendril roots of green things
that would enfold me, grow out of me,
make me mother again.

# Batrachomancy

*divination by frogs*

Somewhere they leap on soft, wet banks,
crouch in clear waters, their mottled skin
as dew-brilliant as the spiderwebs were the spring
my father saved them. They don't know how
they were spared, of course, the wrist-thin skin
of their throats pale and pulsing to sound out
the hours, each other. Perhaps only a few
still survive that spring twelve years ago,
when their mother trekked from the wooded stream
that bordered our yard and emptied her belly
in our swimming pool—nebulous cluster
of milky globules suspended there, each an eye
with its black, pinpricked center. There,
to our spellbound disgust, they hatched—
the pool a frantic bevy of heads and tails,
the luck or curse that placed them there.
If I follow them back through their afterlives,
bellowing and skin-darkened to herald
a coming rain, voluble with warning
when storms approached, some lost,
perhaps tweezed apart in junior high labs,
or caught again by my father, cupped too tightly
in the hands of his new daughter—if I follow them
back through their chorused, forested lives,
I can trace them up the garden hose
that poured them in synchronized frenzy
into their rightful waters, the hose
a sinuous lifeline climbing the yard to our pool,
where its other end siphoned the tadpoles
from a water thrilled with their darting chaos.
Look harder, farther: I see my father
by the stream, kneeling in damp clay,
his lungs full, his mouth around the hose
inhaling a deep, slow gasp, then another,
until the summoned water met his mouth.

The bodies pouring out into the life
they had not known to imagine.
And his watching them arrow away
in the current like undoused green flames.
And the bitter, secret taste on his tongue.

# Exile with Fox

Midnight, mid-May. The earth supple
with three weeks of rain, Queen Anne
lacing the clover, dandelions racing the slope
of hill behind our house.
Our dog noses through yards, puddle-pawed,
until suddenly he is gone—bent to the wild will
of instinct, your gasp and halt call
a hundred feet too slow. Still I glimpse
his tempter, the redly skittish sprint of a fox
just one breath quicker. Poor creature—
chased through the city from one exile
into another, some hedge or damp shed
where he might cower, helpless to snuff
the giveaway glare of his eyes. What was it
we read once?—that one great love is a thing
to be feared because it makes of all others
a kind of exile. Overhead the stars shiver
in their deep cave. To them the chase must
look like a comet, a match blown out.
No, the wind of breath as it first cups the flame.
O love me, fleet tail. Sweet air, streets
memoried with rain. No, not a match
at all: cosmic kaleidoscope, its scrutable tilt.

# Apology

Sunday, halflight. Cooling floors and windowsills.
Across the table I see the drift

of memory in your face—there,
the slight pout and part of your lips
as though to kiss or begin a word.

Some days we do not speak much.

Outside, wasps find gardens, eaves,
even the underside of a child's finger:

his wail rises from a nearby yard.
You, as a boy, once thrust your stung hand
through your pocket, which tore open

like a cloud—pennies and quarters
pouring loose to your socks.

Your finger pulsed with pain, invaded
by a sliver thin as the thread your mother would use
to mend your pocket closed,

your mouth around a curse
(the quick thrill of a forbidden word).

Some days our quiet

is the threatened wasp striking.
And others it is your mother easing

your tender finger into a spoon of milk.
Outside, neighbors shake out tablecloths
and bring the wash in from the line.

A small thing meets our window

with its body, sudden as blood, as affection.

## Hands

I told her to look up
all the definitions of the word
*hand* and choose her favorite one.

—

My favorite:
a unit of measure
equal to four inches
used especially for the height
of horses

—

*This is a stupid prompt,* she says.

This year the fifteen-year-old girls wear
choker necklaces and off-the-shoulder tops
which both go well with that timeless outer layer
of cool dismissal
that protects you from anyone else
suspecting you care too much.

—

I sent her the notebook
because her therapist
and the district attorney
and the guidance counselor
and our mother—everyone tells her to write.
But she cannot write about that.

What I mean to say is
hand it to the page, shift the weight of it
little by little until you don't carry it all.

But what I say is
*Imagine yourself as a flower. What kind of flower would you be?* and
*Make up a knock-knock joke* and
*Imagine the contents of your closet as a city. Who is the mayor?* and
*What do you think is the opposite of "father"? Think hard. You can't say mother.*

—

*Make a list of things that are blue*

<u>My list:</u>
blueberries
a bruise swimming to surface
Virginia mountains
the ring of flame beneath the pan
one line for no baby, two for yes

<u>Her list (as I imagine it):</u>
the sky
Kool-Aid
eyeliner
the veins in my wrist
the lines of this paper

—

Also blue:
the butterflies
my sister draws on her wrist
when really she wants to touch it
with a blade
(fine white scars
marking their tissue wings)

—

If her sorrow were a horse
I would not be able to reach my hands
high enough to measure it, to say,
it is this many hands high,
here is where it ends.

I will have to go on placing one hand,
then the other, careful to touch the heel of one palm
to the crest of my other hand's tallest finger,
repeat, repeat.
Careful not to lose count,
not to let the fierce snorting and stamping of Sorrow
distract me from my task. I place my hands
against the hot sleek coat,
the unbelievable passages of muscle
that ripple beneath my touch.

Eleven, twelve, the tallest horse alive
is twenty hands tall,
but Sorrow is taller. Twenty-one, twenty-two.
I tell my sister when we reach the top,
Sorrow will carry her
to where she wants to go,
they will gallop across the earth.
But we both know

—

We both know Sorrow may outlast us
So we must not lose count
We must not remove our hands

## A Story

In the house a woman touches
everything. The blue rims of plates,
the silk of a shirt, the baby's feather hair.
Light opens the windows in the mornings.
Thistles barb the yard; the clover hums
with bees. There is a man, too. His silence
a language in which the woman
is fluent. A small motor churns
in the house: the baby has learned
to blow raspberries with her lips.
Her spit mists about, forms glass pearls
on her chin and upper lip. She shines,
she is pleased with her way of sounding.
Tonight, in the bedroom, the man will put
his hands in the woman's hair.
The baby will blow raspberries as she moves
through the shifting rooms of sleep.
In this way they all pray in tongues.

# Rent

In the second house we rented—floors slanted,
faucets pearling droplets no matter how
we tightened the knobs—we spent most nights

trying to take back what we'd said. You,
with your set jaw, your untouchable hands,
unable to understand what fury

had just swept through us again. A family
of cardinals built a nest in the thick vine
that coiled and trellised the skeletal parts

of our tilted porch, mezzanines of green.
The nest balanced there, belonging and not,
just inside a crest of vine. The mother,

her blanched yellow head startling apart
the verdure, flew back and forth for weeks
with bits of worm and seed in her beak,

placed these into the insatiable mouths
of her babies. The father swooped in too
to help quiet the voracious chorus.

You laughed when I said these words,
*babies* and *father*, when I crowed
what a good mother she was, what vigilant

watch she kept for any quiver of threat—
namely, me, moving too quick to the door
to watch her. In April the winds picked up—

flourishes of gusts tried our lopsided walls,
whistled through the rusted mail slot
in the water-warped door, even swayed

the streetlights. Sirens pierced the streets.
I worried, crossed the dark and shifting floors
those disquieted nights to know the nest

had weathered the wind, an anchor
of grass and thread sunk in the leaves
that kept it. Until one morning

it hadn't. The vine wind-ripped, askew,
the nest dangling and empty.
For so long I thought the wild out there

was nothing to the wild in here. I was wrong.
*What did you expect?* you asked. But your eyes—
*be devastated,* said your eyes.

# Anniversary

*To love purely is to consent to distance.*
–Simone Weil

The other night you woke me
        to ask who was ringing our doorbell.

*We don't have a doorbell,*
        I replied, and in this way

didn't answer your question.
        (How to love you enough

to speak to your dreams?)
        Once in a strange fluorescent bathroom

we ate chicken wings over double sinks.
        Just you and me and what the mirror

said about us:
        I wore a white blouse,

you bowed your head
        for each bite. (No—the question

is not one of *enough*.) I wish for us to love
        without context, and afterward to cool

in the dark like a modest rubble
        of pale, brittle bones.

To open the door
        and tell the mysterious guest

in the white blouse,
        her finger on the faint bell,

*From now on, just walk in.*

# Lithomancy

*divination by gemstones*

Like eye color or money or even a propensity
to watch TV, we inherit the moment our teeth emerge.
No surprise, then, when I glimpsed the milky white ridge,
half the width of my pinky nail,
splitting my daughter's lower gums at just three months—
exactly when I'd first sprung my own,
my mother told me. Three months:
hardly old enough to grasp a teething ring,
too young for painkillers or to gnaw
a cold strawberry. Baby teeth, milk teeth,
X-Actos in miniature, blades undulled by years
of chew or grind—new-minted, fresh off the line.
By now, months later, she has dragged grooves
in plastic spoons, bitten marks upon her arm
that didn't fade for hours (*She's just figuring out*
*what they do,* my mother said when I called),
nearly drawn blood from my nipple. They sprout in twos,
pushing slowly, tortuously, through the gum,
pink passage from their periodontal underworld
into the light of speech, the open mouth.
The source of distress is invisible at first,
marked only by rivers of drool, a white-seared
tumescence in the mouth, and a keening moan
she performs all day—as she does now, chewing her fingers,
a sure herald of the buds about to bloom.
Mothers around here swear by amber necklaces:
call it voodoo or superstition, or a new science
backed only by anecdotal evidence,
but the amber beads are said to release an oil
into the skin to relieve sore and swollen gums,
the resin-colored gems as small as milk teeth themselves.
When I turn to get my daughter's beads
from the dresser, I see they have fallen in the uncanny shape
of a uterus, even bordered by curling fallopian anterooms.

Remarkable, it stops me, she in the flesh
and this remembrance, the ground of her making,
pictured beside her. Even there, in her former life,
her present distress gestated: the tooth buds
of all primary teeth discernible at eight weeks
after conception, dormant and brooding,
an eruption we watch for. The pain
of the mouth to mature toward language.
Now at seven months she hums when pleased,
exclaims in squeals, makes accidental fricatives,
glissandos her vowels, her mouth filling with order
and precision, white plinths carved from the quarry
of her gums, on which, someday soon,
she'll construct a word. A word like *momma,*
the name of the galaxy from which she came—
her body galactic too, born already with her million eggs,
which begin, steadily, to die,
most never released from the ovary.
So many years ago my mother carried me
and the glint of my daughter
as I carried her, her million glints.
Who else did I carry, pocketed within her,
a mere granule of one of these amber beads?
What are our odds of being named? Of being held?
She runs her tongue along her latest teeth,
tugs a finger at the aching place. A star
inside her blinks out, lost,
as this dawning tooth will soon be—
an absence, only a lisp to whistle
for a while through her words.

# Fontanel

At first I called it her blowhole, shallow lull
in the landscape of her fresh-formed head.
From Old French *fontanel,* it crowned her frontal
lobe. *It freaks me out,* my husband said.

Fountain, soft spot, visible pulse: her blood
surging allegretto. Fountain, yes, at first:
her tears, my milk, my tears: everything flowed.
But hours became days again, her thirst

slowed, her three hundred bones—a lavish excess
that made her pliant, soft, for that slow crush
of being born—disappeared into less.
As she does now, down the stairs, though I rush

to catch her and cannot. From her lip, a gush
of blood: it flows away, as all fountains must.

## Sestets

*with a line by Simone Weil*

1.

Two forces rule the universe: light & gravity.

The child fills the mother's belly,
suspended as a winged thing in the web of her ribs.

Sunlight passes through her skin:
                                                                the luminaria world of shape & shift.

Afloat, he turns, turns,
                                                  until her pelvis is his crown.
Defiant, now: but loosening in his heavy cloud.

2.

*Uppgivenhetssyndrom*

In Sweden, refugee children denied asylum
sometimes slip into an unwakeable sleep for months.
We have no word for this in English. Not *sleep* because no rest.
Not *coma* because no disease, no harm to the body.
Put them by windows, the doctors say, let the light enter their skin
& wind the circadian clock of their exile.

3.

Twilight. The pines saw the light in half
& nail it to the grass. I walk the planks
beneath the nascent cones, opaline in their sap caul

& drop to my knees to search. Two forces rule the universe:
light & gravity. My grassblade sift yields this seed—
daughter's tooth—pink cling of its broken root.

4.

A dragonfly moves in cursive
over the flaming stalks of tiger lilies.

*Tigers willies,* she repeats. Her soft halation of hair
is the crayon sun I drew for her—

not light, not fire, not filament—

just a bright, brief scribbling on the air.

5.

Each night my voice becomes the light
                                                        that ferries her
into the dark of sleep. *You are my sunshine, my only sunshine...*

It takes eight minutes & twenty seconds for sunlight to reach earth.
By this time
                  her eyes are closed,

her breath pulled along in the deep undertow of dreams,
that other gravity to which we surrender our lives.

# The Spinning Place

> *Thomas Stevens took a giant spin, becoming the first person to complete a trip around earth by bicycle.*
>
> –*The New York Times*

Sometime on the third day of Hungary
she joins him. Day and night, day
and night, propelled by the will of his legs,

he has been alone. Until now.
She is light and deft, a quixotic velocity.
She points at churches, at gypsies,

laughs and floods the unraveling road
with a language he cannot understand.
The inflection of asking lifts the hem

of her words. To him each note in her
impossible tongue asks, *What are you afraid of?*
*When will you live in one city again?*

Above them, a hawk spirals and dips. To it the world
is a brambled field, each day as simple as the hunt
for what invisible feet tunnel there.

He sees the twentieth century loom before them.
Buildings rise and fall. Great crowds cross
borders. Capitals change names. Calls of birds

go extinct. *There are no cities,* he says, *only this*
*pedaled cartography of unbelonging.*
The blue distills into granules of stars

and the air is hymnic, honeyed
with last light. He has not said what he meant.
She turns to go back the way

they came, the distance between them unspooled
and irrevocable, held in place by the flash
of spinning spokes, that bright and restless carousel.

# The Spellbound Horses

Their coats creekbright so that
I can nearly see myself

in the afterstorm ecstasy of the sun
the world unlocked flung

open dripping and verdant
They do not blink or move

their barn scattered in planks
blasted apart about the ravaged

yard What terror
to be spared or resurrected

For weeks after you emerged
from me unhoused

you'd wake from sleep the large indigo
of your eyes stunned

What to say when a world ends
*Hello* I'd tell you

*hello* gently not to startle
*everything is still broken*

You the dreamer I the dream
my face like one underwater

parceled by light just after
the funnel has let go of earth

## —*Fields of Praise*—

# Duet

1. *Hurt*

The spaded earth spurts in fury:
a geyser of yellow jackets torque

from their lair. You come inside,
stung, from the dervish

of small commas
they make of the air.

2. *Coda*

You of the thrumming
pierced ear, come here—

let me compose these wishbone
tweezers in the air

above the eyelash dash that breaks
the line of your ear.

In the next room,
our daughter, tiptoed upon

her rickety blue chair,
composes one finger in the air,

choosing a black or white key
upon which to alight.

Make a wish.
C-sharp.

Impossible to say (a lesson
in touch) who stings who.

# Lullaby in a Drought

In the drawers, in the cabinets,
we find pecan casings and pellets,

the answer to the question
of what patters in the walls at night.

We are not the only lovers here.
If the lights go out, we used to say,

you pour the wine and I'll find
the matches. But we dare not tempt them

in this tinder town—where sycamores shed
parched unready leaves, where yards are fringed

with thistle barbs. If the waters rise,
we used to say, you pour the wine

and I'll tear out the best pages.
But now the baby's in her seventh week,

pulled from the secret waters
of my body into a rainless topography.

Who is more sorry?
She sleeps the sleep of rivers.

In the nights I sit cradleside when she wakes,
humming Brahms' famous notes—

a song he wrote to sway an old love.
So we are always singing

what we cannot change.
The walls fill with patter, rain clouds

form somewhere else. The wine
grows older, finer. If the funnel forms,

if the hail falls.

# Hope

For a while my mother left notes,
one on each stair, in the hope
that if my father came home he'd follow them,
some compulsory trail, up to where she slept.
*Remember Asheville,* they might say,
or *Please can you make some sweet tea? Nobody else*
*makes it like you do,* or simply his name.
An arrow pointing to the next step.
My sister and I found them unbearable,
the baldness of her pain too bright
to look at. We buttered toast in the mornings,
made sandwiches for school, bad sweet tea
we carried up to her in the afternoons.
Hope is like that sometimes.
We said if we ever left that house
we'd take the pictures off the walls
but strew the nails across the stairs.
We imagined the prick, the dewdrop of blood,
the *O* of his startled mouth in the hollow house.
And even then we wanted that pain
for ourselves—a pain we could point to,
that would interrupt our lives.
A pain that would come as surprise.

# In Praise of the Names of Things

My daughter knows around thirty words
and some of them are animal sounds,
though the doctor assures me that counts.
She's very good at onomatopoeia.
When the neighbor's Great Dane charged
up and down his length of fence
barking at her, his body electric with muscle,
the air thunderous with his fury,
she stood very still, watching him,
and only replied, *woof.*
*Dog,* she says, when the squirrel runs
up the tree. *Dog,* when she spots the large elk
moving quietly through the white woods.
*Moon!* she says, pointing at each streetlight.
*Water* is everywhere: the toilet, the sink,
the hot pot, the mud puddle.
Some water we can touch and some we can't.
I struggle to tell her the truth. That is a *dog.*
(But it's a puppy.) See its feet? (Paws)
Touch its hair. (Fur) See, he likes you!
(He wants to taste the fine frost
of sugar mantling your upper lip.)
When she wakes each morning, she sits in her crib
practicing her words—
making sure they're all still there.
*Momma, baby, baa baa, rock, walk, book.*
When I told my students monosyllabic words
force us to slow down, they did not
believe me. No, they said, that's just Augustine's *style.*
But see how I slow outside her door to hear
the careful curation, the strung litany of sounds
that places her in the world. In my world.
In a world with such good things
as dogs and moons, and moondogs,
which I'll explain someday,

pointing at that luminous halo,
its two rare bright beads.
Scuff marks on the floor of heaven.
Smudged breath spots on the oculus
that looks into a beyond
we're still working to name.
(Ice crystals refracted by light.
More water we can't touch.)

# Via Negativa

She opens a book
& with her tongue
makes a kind of repetitive
*L* sound, though this is
only partly true, since
her sounds are still free
& wild, unscaffolded
by alphabets. It is like
*L*, but not. *What does*
*a dog say?* I ask her,
though at the same time
I wonder who decided
babies should learn
animal sounds
right away, before even
*help* or *yes*. She replies
with something like
*thwack*. She points out
the window & blurts
a sound that starts
with *B* & somehow rhymes
with *push* & *mirage*.
Her babbles are little
mirages of words:
they shimmer with
meaning & substance
but disappear
into the ether
between her mouth
& my ear. Her mirage
language will one day
very soon be lost,
word for word replaced
with my imperial coaxing:
*dog, milk, book*.

Some say silence
is the truest form
of prayer, but I think
it is this: she speaks
and does not mean
to mean. She knows
her voice will turn
my face to her.

# The Reader

*after Richard Wilbur*

I confess that more than once
I have tried to hide the book
about *the old house in Paris*
*that was covered in vines,*
knowing as I do that each night
it will be her choice. She slides
the hard green volume from the shelf
and hugs it to herself, a book
the size of her own ribcage,
declaring, *Madeline is heavy!*
We settle in together for our return
to 1930s Paris (our bodies sharing
a perimeter as they once shared
everything), the wounded soldier
with the broken leg for whom
the girls are sad (*He broked*
*his leg,* she says on cue).
The tale of fearless, smallest Madeline
has become a script, her favorite.
At her age she finds, every day,
that for each word she knows
there are twenty she does not,
the language swelling, moving away
from her like a cosmos not bound
to her small gravity—
but here is a collection of words
that never changes, each one
where she left it, a Pompeii
of sounds and pictures.
Nothing could be more right
than her patient, page-turning
anticipation to interject, just in time,
Ms. Clavel's nocturnal epiphany:
*Something is not right!*

Please, pick a different book,
I've pleaded, but she is devoted
to this story, and devotion—
its familiarities, its threadbare habits
of love—is new to her, too.
So stay where you are, Madeline,
I append, for soon enough
it is she who will be changed,
returning to you much later to find
you still dismiss the tiger in the zoo,
still daydream the plaster crack
into a rabbit on the ceiling.
She will return with the other girls
to bring you a flower, but find
instead a new kinship
with your body's boast of scar
(her mother's voice become an architecture
of shade that lengthens away
from the words, each one
opened again in its crypt of ash).

# Drop-Off

Just as I'm leaving,
after three more
*one more kisses*, your teacher
pulls the alarm. Fire
Safety Week. You and the other
two-year-olds file out,
singing the fire truck song.
Every week on the news
a man has taken
his gun and his plan
somewhere new.
This morning you asked
for a blue bow—not pink—
and your blonde hair
splays around it now,
a ribbon paperweight
against the wind.
The alarm sounds the drama
of flame, and you enact
your escape pageant
to the far reach of the play area,
where all wiggling ten of you
line against the chain link fence
and your teacher points
a camera, calling *smile*,
for the Fire Safety Wall.
In the movie you love
about the Great Barrier Reef
the father fish warns his son
to stay away from the drop-off
lest he be taken or lost.
The father is neurotic
and right. The son is taken.
I wonder how many bullets
can fit through the eyelet
barrier of that fence.

I should run
to the fence and scream
that you'd all be safer
in the fire
and kiss you one more time.
Instead I pray
it will always be a rehearsal.
Instead I know
it will not, and I drive
away anyway. In seven hours,
when I return, you show me
the picture you colored of fire,
orange and yellow and wet
with red, the paper torn through
in three places where you pressed
so hard, so happy,
that it broke.

# A Stubborn Ode

*after Jack Gilbert*

All of it. Somewhere girls being herded
at gunpoint into vans. The violence
of the housefly toward the window.
A man in kerosene clothes
touching the flame to himself.
The child calling her mother's name until it is no longer
a word, but a pulse, unrelenting.
Kyler's upturned face intent, rapt—his mitt
compelling him sideways to catch the ball
thrown by the second father to come into his life.
The brazenness of saying one pain is like another.
The inferno of California valleys. A pastor mouthing the name
of his God in a prison. The plane somewhere
and all the bones accounted for. The small colony
of tree lobsters living on an island of rock
in the Tasman Sea, surviving eighty years
on one plant. Believed extinct. Flightless.

# Early Resurrections (News from the Week)

A man broke out of the county jail.
Reports list him as barefoot and still cuffed.
Wednesday of Holy Week and *alleluia*
has not been uttered in this town for nearly forty days.
A wounded opossum limps down the sidewalk,
its graceful glitch returning to me
when the knife slips as I put it to the bread—
my finger instead—and my love hurries
to part the wound, red buttonhole in my skin,
to see its depth. Yesterday in the garden
I saw a silkmoth had failed to spin its whole cocoon—
but without its cirrus, monastic piñata,
it went on transforming anyway,
nearly clear wings nubile, jade,
tucked into themselves.
Could we have watched?—the stone
heaved away, the angel not yet dispatched,
the body still softly scarring, untrue,
untouchable, its grief flinching from our eyes.
As handcuffs glint in a glade
in their stolen slice of light.
When I saw the secret of the silkmoth, I confess—
*alleluia* burned on my tongue.

## Shoulder

She flies south to visit me
though it is deep summer.

Curved in ink
up her hind left shoulder—

its fine filaments splayed
as though in wind-riled disarray—

a solitary plume.

—

Curved in ink—
needle ink. Jade ink, violet.

Emerald, black.
Indelible accoutrement

to her camisole's silk strap,
the peacock feather's eye

will not blink back.
Wielded ink, truth-or-dare ink,

it stalks me, brazen,
will not unmeet my shy eye.

I close my eyes: the afterimage
is green glare, flash of sun

succumbing to horizon.

—

Truth-or-dare ink.
Truth: in a tattoo parlor,
you can choose your pain,
tell it where to go, what to be.

Dare: against our mother's counsel,
she's new in her skin

for the second time,
flesh welted red and tender,

the hurt of what it took to arrive here—
in time, in body—

already vestigial and dwindling still,
like sun-blanked, rain-rinsed

chalk ebbing back into sidewalk,
the last blue silt carried off

in a sudden wind.

—

Vestigial and dwindling still,
the sear of late light solves

her shirt's thin cotton
as she walks away from me—

a parsed wing silhouetted there,
faint as shadow, and as fixed.

# SEPTEMBER PSALM

*Valparaiso University*

It's summer's last call,
the sky electric coral in the evenings,
then ashen pink, then a final pale pucker
as bats dart beneath lights.
This is the hour of the erasers,
come to ghost the classrooms
with a little humming, some water
sloshed from a pail,
and the great unwriting begins.
They absolve midterm dates,
cancel Gettysburg, erode the ribs
of the human skeleton.
They unstack the kindling
of the music staff, halve the half notes,
unconjugate *cantar*.
The erasers thumb their rosary
of rooms and walk out
beneath a chalk moon.
The sky is a sill of dust.
Beneath it, the stadium shudders
with a primal chorus,
which rises toward the towering lights,
where a thick cloud of moths
clots against a brilliance
they can neither resist nor keep.

# While Shopping for a Mattress

Impossible not to think of nights
you won't sleep at all, your restless body beside me,
nights your feet are light as the moon
on the floors of our house—
though the salesman's nearing face,
his calling out do we like the extra-firm,
why not just *try* the king size, see if
we wouldn't like more space,
makes it harder to wonder at our lives
passing in dreams, in sex, in what we murmur
in the last minute of the last hour
we are awake each day, wonder if there will be
many nights you turn off the lamp
without a word exchanged between us,
my shoulders angled away from you,
and no, I do not want more space,
a bed is not meant to be a field
but a garden, which is why
it too is called *bed,* and I want
to be beside you as floribundas
are beside tea roses, close enough
so that in full bloom their edges touch—
how not to think of the smaller bodies
our bodies will sow in other beds,
our one mattress become two, three
other mattresses we will need to buy—
but now you are rising, moving toward
that pillowtop in the window,
and though I am sad to leave
the life in which we are roses, I see
in your neck, the span of your shoulders,
where the years will soften you,
pull you toward another sleep,
a current you cannot refuse,
and because I promised, I follow you
through the store and lie beside you
into the years of sleep we will choose,
even into the one we will not.

# Fixing the Foot

*after Philip Levine*

She follows me out of the bathroom,
I'm sort of lurching sideways
with every step, trying not to press the ball
of my foot to the floor—
a granule of glass glints in that callous of skin.
She is quiet, all of a sudden, the kinetic quiet
of a toddler's observation, her small soft face
grave with witness to my agitation.
A new thing unfolds before her—
her mother wounded, discomposed.
She follows me through the house,
the sinking sun slanted in shards
along the treacherous floor. At last
we come to her father, and I sit,
without a word, and hand him the tweezers.
He takes my foot in his kind hand.
She watches, rapt and still, her eyes
on my face, his face, his hands,
the offending spark pulled free.
Hardly bigger than two grains of sugar,
or a diamond in a wedding band.
And pink, now, from its blood plunge,
its brief stay in my body.
*What's daddy doing?* she finally asks.
And what is the word for this?—
A lovely thing the body turns to pain.

## The Spinning Place

They billow up from warm estuarial waters,
        blooming toward that brilliant, ever-shattering pane.
So many manatees—the ones that are left—
        already bear the marks of this collision, the touching
of one world to another. Water to sky. Vault to vault.
        The elephantine flesh of their backs
is slashed and hatched, indelible history
        of what it takes to breathe. They billow up

toward shifting islands of shade: boats hover
        on the face of the deep, indistinguishable from cloud shadow.
There, carving water from water, propellers spin
        and do not flinch from flesh. But the creature's need
can be met only where two worlds meet,
        at the bright seam that holds them together
and apart. So gored, bleeding, they descend again,
        lungs full, with breath enough in their wounds to sing.

# Acknowledgments

Thank you to Michael Waters for believing in this book. To Ron Mitchell for the Mega Bloks and for being such a delightful editor, a champion of the work of others: I'm endlessly grateful for you.

For giving me two wonderful years to work on this manuscript, I owe a debt of gratitude to the Lilly Fellows Program in Humanities and the Arts. My deepest, abiding gratitude to Mark Schwehn, Dorothy Bass, and Joe Creech. For being such brilliant, inspiring, and gracious friends, thank you to Elizabeth Fredericks, Patrick Gardner, Ashleigh Elser, and Daniel Silliman. Thank you to Kjerstin Kauffman for insight on many of these poems in earlier versions.

To my teachers: thank you to Corey Marks, Bruce Bond, and B.H. Fairchild, who offered advice on many of these poems—and this manuscript—in its earlier versions.

To John Ruff, mentor, friend, fellow poet, thank you.

And finally, thank you to my children for teaching me how to speak all over again; and to Mark, my heart, my very best thought: thank you for your words and your life.

My thanks to the journals in which some of these poems first appeared:

*32 Poems*: "Solstice" & "The Spinning Place" (III)
*The Arkansas International*: "Anniversary" & "Sestets"
*Birmingham Poetry Review*: "My Sister Sketches Her Anorexia"
*Boulevard*: "Hands"
*Cave Wall*: "Fontanel" & "Night Shift"
*Copper Nickel*: "September Psalm"
*Crab Orchard Review*: "Poison"
*Crazyhorse*: "The Spinning Place" (I)
*The Cresset*: "Prelude to Circulatory System" & "Via Negativa"
*Hawk & Handsaw*: "Batrachomancy" & "Lullaby in a Drought"
*JuxtaProse*: "Apology"
*Image*: "Advent," "Duet," "Exile with Fox" & "Scale"
*Meridian*: "Miscarriage" & "While Shopping for a Mattress"

*Michigan Quarterly Review*: "Delivery Room (Sacrament Under Erasure)"

*The Normal School*: "A Story" & "Lithomancy"

*North American Review*: "Rent"

*Plume*: "Shoulder"

*Poetry Northwest*: "Exile (The Spellbound Horses)" & "The Spellbound Horses"

*Salt Hill*: "A Stubborn Ode"

*The Southeast Review*: "Hope"

*Southern Indiana Review*: "Fixing the Foot" & "In Praise of the Names of Things"

*Southern Poetry Review*: "Annunciation (While Pregnant, I Develop Aviophobia)"

*The Southern Review*: "Early Resurrections (News from the Week)," "The Reader" & "The Spinning Place" (II)

*Stirring*: "Descent (Sort of an Annunciation)," "Drop-Off" & "Lines Approaching a Birthday"

Photo by Edward Byrne

Chelsea Wagenaar is the author of *Mercy Spurs the Bone,* selected by Philip Levine as the 2013 winner of the Philip Levine Prize. She holds a BA from the University of Virginia and a PhD from the University of North Texas. Her work has appeared in *The Southern Review, Gulf Coast, Crazyhorse,* and many others. Wagenaar teaches at Valparaiso University in Indiana, where she lives with her husband, Mark, and their two children.

The Michael Waters Poetry Prize was established in 2013 to honor Michael's contributions to *Southern Indiana Review* and American arts and letters.

## MWPP Winners

2018—Chelsea Wagenaar

2017—Marty McConnell

2016—Ruth Awad

2015—Annie Kim

2014—Dennis Hinrichsen & Hannah Faith Notess

2013—Doug Ramspeck